BFF or NRF?

(Not Really Friends)

A Girl's Guide To Happy Friendships

To the girls who shared their voices and opened their hearts to bring this book to life. And to my daughters, who provided guidance and wisdom every step of the way. *May you hold fast to courage and let your true self shine bright.*

—J.S.

Published by Familius LLC, www.familius.com

Familius books are available at special discounts for bulk purchases, whether for sales promotions or for family or corporate use. For more information, email orders@familius.com.

Reproduction of this book in any manner, in whole or in part, without written permission of the publisher is prohibited.

Library of Congress Control Number: 2021933763

Print ISBN 9781641701952

Ebook ISBN 9781641703697

Printed in the United States of America

Illustrations by Elowyn Dickerson

Edited by Kaylee Mason, Peg Sandkam, and Brooke Jorden

Cover design by Emma Hiatt

Book design by Carlos Guerrero

10 9 8 7 6 5 4 3 2 1

First Edition

BFF or NRF?

(Not Really Friends)

A Girl's Guide To Happy Friendships

FAMILIUS

CONTENTS

INTRODUCTION

If you've struggled in a friendship, you're not alone. Most girls find that, sometimes, friendship feels like a roller coaster. One moment you're climbing through fun and laughter; the next, you're plunging into fear or frustration.

Friendships are amazing, but they can also be confusing and hard. Maybe friendship drama makes school more frustrating than fun? Or possibly it seems that everyone has a BFF but you? Or you and your friend spend more time arguing than agreeing?

The good news is that friendship doesn't have to be such a bumpy ride. In fact, healthy friendships feel safe and accepting. Yes, there are still bumps here and there, but strong friendships work through these bumps together.

Just like learning anything new, friend-ship skills take practice. This book explores the different levels of friendship, from Close Friends to NRFs (Not Really Friends), as well as skills to help smooth out the ride. So grab a pencil and let's get started!

Super-Duper Important:

This book uses the pronouns "she/her," but feel free to change the pronouns to fit you and your friendships when doing the book's activities.

To protect privacy, names and story details have been changed.

Chapter 1

QUIZ: HOW HEALTHY ARE MY FRIENDSHIPS?

BFF, bestie, buddy—there are many ways to describe friends. But what really makes a "good" or "close" friend? And why do some friendships feel like a cozy robe, while others feel like a scary movie?

Sometimes we can figure out if a friendship is healthy or not by noticing how we feel after spending time with that friend. For example, if spending time with Keisha usually leaves you feeling happy and good about yourself, while spending time with Hazel leaves you feeling sad or confused, your friendship with Keisha is probably healthier.

The following quiz will help you gain a better understanding of which of your friendships are healthy and which may need some work.

Quiz Instructions: Think of <u>one friend</u> as you read through the quiz and mark the best responses. Be sure to answer honestly so you get a true understanding of that friendship. Take the quiz over again for as many friends as you would like.

Super-Duper Important:

Keep your responses to the quiz private or share only with a trusted adult. This quiz is intended for your personal awareness and should not be used to criticize or judge others.

Quiz: How Healthy Is My Friendship?

• • •• •• •• •• •• •• •• •• •• •• •• •• •• •• •• •• •• •• • •

	Almost Always	Sometimes	Almost Never
When problems come up in our friendship, we find a way to work it out that feels fair.	☐	☐	☐
If I share a secret with my friend, I know she'll keep it. She doesn't say mean things about others behind their backs.	☐	☐	☐
I can share my thoughts and feelings with my friend, and she won't make fun of me or make me feel bad.	☐	☐	☐

	Almost Always	Sometimes	Almost Never
After we spend time together, I feel happy and good about myself.	☐	☐	☐
When I share a big accomplishment, my friend is happy for me. She doesn't use that moment to share something she did better.	☐	☐	☐
If my friend does or says something mean to me, she takes responsibility and apologizes. Her apology feels sincere, and I know she'll try not to make the same mistake again.	☐	☐	☐

	Almost Always	Sometimes	Almost Never
My friend supports my interests and goals, even if they're different from hers.	☐	☐	☐
My friend doesn't feel jealous or threatened when others join our activities. She doesn't make me feel bad if I spend time with other friends.	☐	☐	☐
I know my friend would stand up for me.	☐	☐	☐
Our friendship is equal. I'm not always the leader or the follower.	☐	☐	☐

Quiz Results: How Healthy Is My Friendship?

If you marked...

8 or More "Almost Always":

Congratulations, this sounds like a healthy friendship! This friendship feels safe and accepting. You can share your thoughts and feelings with this friend because she's kind and respectful. And this friendship feels balanced because you listen to each other's ideas and work together to find fair solutions to problems.

Note: If this description does not fit your friendship, double-check your responses. Maybe this friendship fits more into the "Sometimes" description below.

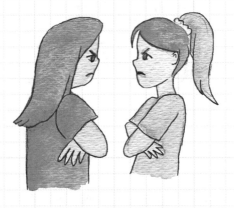

3 or More "Sometimes":

No friendship is perfect, but if several of your responses were "Sometimes," this friendship may need some work. Possibly you and this friend can improve sharing feelings, listening, and supporting each other. The "Speaking Up in Friendships" chapter of this book (page 75) will help with communicating and problem solving. See if you can get a better understanding of what each of you might be doing or not doing that is keeping this friendship from feeling really good.

3 or More "Almost Never":

Caution! This friendship may not be healthy, which means it doesn't feel safe and accepting. If time with this friend often leaves you feeling sad, frustrated, or bad about yourself, it's time to begin speaking up to improve this friendship (page 75) or moving on and growing the friendships that light you up rather than deflate you. Taking a break from this friend may be difficult if you've known each other for a long time. The "Making New Friends" (page 109) and "Taking Care of Myself" (page 115) chapters of this book will help as you decide the best path for you.

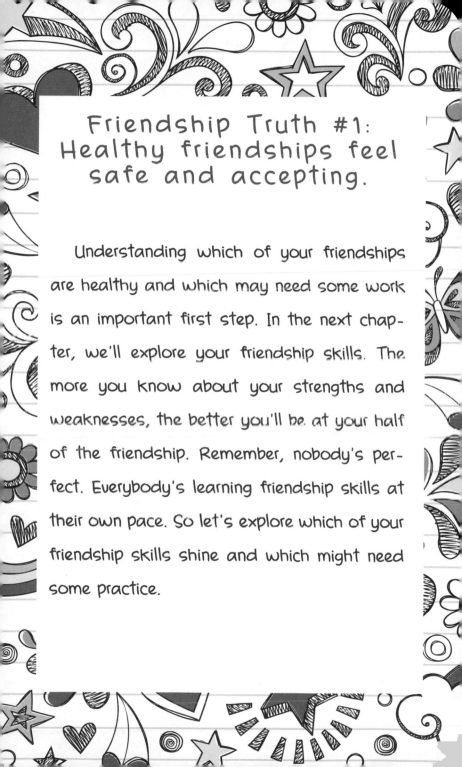

Friendship Truth #1: Healthy friendships feel safe and accepting.

Understanding which of your friendships are healthy and which may need some work is an important first step. In the next chapter, we'll explore your friendship skills. The more you know about your strengths and weaknesses, the better you'll be at your half of the friendship. Remember, nobody's perfect. Everybody's learning friendship skills at their own pace. So let's explore which of your friendship skills shine and which might need some practice.

Chapter 2

Quiz: How Are My Friendship Skills?

Have you ever noticed that some things are easy for you to do and other things are hard? Maybe drawing pictures feels easy to you, but playing soccer feels hard. Or solving math problems feels easy, but writing stories feels hard.

We all have skills that come easily to us and others that are harder to learn. Luckily, we can improve any skill with practice.

Everyone has different friendship skills too. Some friendship skills may feel easy for you, like listening to others, while other skills may feel hard, such as not sharing gossip.

The following quiz will help you get a better understanding of your unique friendship skills. Remember, nobody's perfect. This quiz will help you better understand yourself, which of your friendship skills are strong, and which skills could use some practice.

Quiz Instructions: Think of how you act in your friendships as you read through the quiz and mark either TRUE or FALSE. Be sure to be honest, so you get a true understanding of yourself.

Keep your responses to the quiz private or share only with a trusted adult. This quiz is intended for your self-awareness and should not be used to criticize or judge yourself.

Quiz: How Are My Friendship Skills?

Part A

	True This mostly describes me!	False This is harder for me to do.
I try hard not to interrupt when my friend is talking. I let others tell their own stories and jokes.	☐	☐
I'm interested in my friend's activities and life and ask questions to learn more.	☐	☐
When talking with my friend, I try to make sure that sometimes I'm the talker and sometimes I'm the listener, so our conversations feel balanced.	☐	☐

Part B

	True This mostly describes me!	False This is harder for me to do.
I know it's healthy for my friend to have other friends too.	☐	☐
I don't make my friend feel bad for not being with me. Even best friends need some time to be alone or with other friends.	☐	☐
When something really good happens to my friend instead of me, I may feel sad or jealous inside, but I do my best to show my happiness for her.	☐	☐

●● ●● ●● ●● ●● ●● ●● ●● ●● ●● ●● ●● ●● ●● ●● ●● ●● ●● ●

Part C

	True	False
	This mostly describes me!	This is harder for me to do.
I respect my friends' differences. I don't make others feel bad for acting or being different.	☐	☐
I make others feel welcome in my group or activities.	☐	☐
If my friends share their feelings or something important with me, I'm careful not to make fun of or criticize them.	☐	☐

Part D

	True This mostly describes me!	False This is harder for me to do.
If my friend shares a secret with me, I don't share it with others. (*Unless the secret is about an unsafe situation, then I tell an adult.*)	☐	☐
I don't talk about my friends or others in a bad way, especially when they're not there.	☐	☐
If I tell my friend that I'm going to do something, like meet them after school, I make sure I do it.	☐	☐

Part E

	True This mostly describes me!	False This is harder for me to do.

I'm honest about my feelings and I'm able to listen to my friend's feelings too.

☐ ☐

I try to understand my friend's perspective on things, which might be different from mine.

☐ ☐

If something's really bothering me in my friendship, I try to talk one-on-one with my friend to resolve the problem. Or, if I need support, I know talking to a trusted adult is a better choice than involving other friends in the conflict.

☐ ☐

Part F

	True This mostly describes me!	False This is harder for me to do.

I try to think before I speak. When I realize what I'm about to say is mean, I don't say it. I'm respectful, even during conflicts.
☐ ☐

I don't put others down to make myself feel better.
☐ ☐

I try to use a calm tone of voice instead of a mean tone. I know that how I say things is as important as the words I say.
☐ ☐

Part G

I realize that nobody's perfect. I'm open to work-ing on friendship skills and talking through conflicts.
☐ ☐

	True This mostly describes me!	False This is harder for me to do.
My friendships feel equal; I'm not always the leader or always the one making decisions.	☐	☐
I try to work out problems with my friends and find a solution that feels fair to both.	☐	☐

Part H

I don't make up little lies about myself. I like myself as I am and don't need to make things up to sound better or more interesting.	☐	☐
I try hard to tell the truth and to be honest with my friends.	☐	☐

•• •• •• •• •• •• •• •• •• •• •• •• •• •• •• •• •• •• •

Part I

	True This mostly describes me!	False This is harder for me to do.
When I don't win a game, I'm a good sport and congratulate others.	☐	☐
When things don't go my way in my friendships, I try not to stomp off, shout at my friends, or pout. When I'm frustrated, I try to handle my frustration in healthy ways.	☐	☐

Quiz Results: How are my friendship skills?

Friendship skills take practice. Remember, everybody has some skills that come easily and others that take more effort. If you responded FALSE to any question, read the summary below for that part of the quiz.

Super-Duper
Important:

Our actions are a *choice*. We have the power to change our behaviors if we want to. For example, if we have a habit of lying, we have the power to change that. Or if we have a habit of talking behind backs and putting others down, we have the power to stop. It just takes our attention and practice!

Part A: Good Listener

"I get so excited to talk that I interrupt my friends a lot. I'm trying to be a better listener and not interrupt so much, but it's hard." –Brittany

"I'm pretty quiet. I'm a really good listener, but I didn't realize that by not saying anything, my friends didn't know I was listening. Now I try to ask them questions so I can learn about them and show that I care." –Kat

Listening shows your friends that you care about them and what they have to say. Sometimes we get so excited about what we want to say, we forget to listen to the person talking to us. Can you think of a time when you were talking to a friend and they didn't seem to be listening to you? How did that feel?

How can you improve your listening skills (for example, making eye contact, asking questions, putting your phone away, nodding, trying not to interrupt)?

Part B: Managing Jealousy

"I used to get really mad at my best friend when she hung out with somebody else. I thought friends were always supposed to be together. Once I even told her I wouldn't be her friend anymore if she stayed friends with this other girl." –Ahni

"Whenever my friend told me something good that happened to her, I always tried to come up with something better that happened to me. I realize now that's really annoying and I just congratulate her." –Piper

Sometimes we feel jealous if our friend is spending time with others because, deep inside, we may be worried about losing the friendship. Or we may feel jealous about a friend's success and wish that success had been our own. Be careful, jealousy can destroy friendships!

Everyone feels jealous sometimes, but it's important to manage jealousy in healthy ways. To work through jealous feelings, notice when you're feeling jealous and pause. In these moments, remind yourself that healthy friendships allow friends to spend time with other friends. Or, if you're feeling jealous because of others' accomplishments or qualities, remind yourself of your unique qualities. Going for a jog, dancing to your favorite song, or doing something active also helps release tough emotions.

How can you manage jealous feelings in healthy ways (for example, pausing before you speak, reminding yourself of your positive qualities, avoiding comparing yourself to others)?

Part C: Accepting

"Last year, I wasn't nice to some girls in my class. If I didn't like them, I thought that being mean would keep them away from me. Now I try to be respectful to all the kids in my class, even the ones I don't like very much." –Mattie

"I used to hang out with a group that I could tell didn't really like me. I tried to fit in, but I usually felt ignored. Now I have some friends that really accept me. These friendships feel so much better, like I'm really part of this group." –Fatima

Being accepting means allowing others to be themselves and making them feel included. Some kids might accept some friends but reject others because they're different or because they don't like them as much.

Friendships that lack acceptance don't feel very good because you feel like you can't be yourself. Can you think of a friend that really accepts you for who you are? What's it like to be around this friend? How can you practice being more accepting?

Part D: **Trustworthy**

"I used to share my friend's secrets. I think I did this because it helped me feel close to other girls and fit in. My friend stopped being my friend, and I don't blame her. Luckily, I have a new friend now and I'm trying really hard to be trustworthy." –Harper

"Last year, all we did at lunch was gossip about other kids. It seemed like the cool thing to do, but it made me really uncomfortable. My mom suggested I change the subject to more positive stuff. That really helped." –Shanee

Trust means more than keeping secrets. Friendships filled with trust feel really support-ive. When there's trust in a friendship, you feel safe talking about things that are important to you without fear that your friend will make fun of you or tell others. This sense of trust makes these friendships feel special.

Friendships that lack trust often feel unsafe. Feelings get hurt, gossip and secrets are shared, making these relationships confusing too. Trustworthy friendships take time to find and develop, so they might not happen until middle school or later. In the meantime, just work on being trustworthy yourself. What can you do to be a trustworthy friend?

Part E: Good Communicator

"My best friend and I almost stopped being friends because we didn't know how to solve problems. We'd get in fights and then get our other friends to take sides. But then we came up with a way to talk to each other instead of creating drama. It's sometimes hard, but we work out our problems together now. This has made us better friends too." –Lucia

"I have a hard time sharing my feelings. If my friend hurts my feelings, I'm too afraid to say anything. But by not saying anything, the situation doesn't get any better." –Andi

Many girls find it hard to speak up in friendships when there's a problem. If something's bothering you, it might be hard to know what to say to make the situation better. But we teach others how we'd like to be treated. If we don't speak up when something really matters to us, nothing will change. Review the "Speaking Up in Friendships" chapter of this book (page 75) if speaking up is hard for you. Friends work through problems one-on-one and try not to involve others in the conflict. At first, this can feel really hard, but it gets easier with practice and will improve your friendships for a lifetime. How can you practice good communication in your friendships?

Part F: Kind & Respectful

"When I was in sixth grade, a few kids called me mean. This really hurt my feelings. I know I'm not mean, but sometimes I might seem mean because I'm not careful with my words." –Angelica

"When I was little, I used to say everything I thought. Like, if I thought a friend's shirt was ugly, I would tell them that. Now I try to be respectful and think before I talk." –Avery

"When I do kind things and help others, it helps me feel good about myself." –Crystal

Showing kindness and respect to someone means you act in a way that shows you care about their feelings and well-being. Kindness is key to all of our friendships. Acts of kindness can be simple, like saying something encouraging or holding the door open for somebody. When we choose kind words and actions, it makes the world a better place and helps us feel happy too! How can you practice kindness and respect in your friendships?

Part G: Flexible

"Everyone used to call me bossy. I hated it. But now I know why. When I had a really good idea for a game, I had a hard time going with somebody else's idea. My teacher showed me some ways to be flexible, like taking turns or rock, paper, scissors. It really helped." –Morgan

"I really hate being 'it' in tag, so I used to change the rules to get my way. This really made my friends mad and took the fun out of the game. I'm getting better at being flexible now so everybody enjoys the game." –Amber

Time with friends requires a lot of cooperation and problem solving. Deciding what game to play or choosing the rules can feel really frustrating when one friend isn't flexible.

Flexibility means working through choices and conflicts in a way that feels fair to both friends. This is a tricky skill, but with practice, it makes time with friends much more fun. How can you practice being more flexible in your friendships?

Part H: Honest

"Sometimes I make up stories about myself. I like to make people laugh and impress them. But later, when my friends find out my stories aren't true, I get really embarrassed." –Sophia

"I have a friend that sometimes lies to make herself sound better. I wish she'd be more honest because I think she's great just the way she is." –Imani

Sometimes people make things up about themselves to fit in or impress others. Although little lies may seem harmless, they keep us from being true to ourselves. And when we're not true to ourselves, we're not treating ourselves with respect. If you tell stories about yourself that aren't true, think about when you tend to do this and why. How can you stay true to yourself and be more honest in these situations?

Part I: Positive Attitude

"When things didn't go my way when I played games with friends, I used to get really mad. Then I wouldn't let myself have any fun because that would make me look wrong." –Eva

"I have a really positive friend. She's always encouraging and looks on the bright side of things. Being around her makes me want to be more positive too." –Brittany

It's frustrating when things don't go the way we want them to. It's perfectly okay to be mad, but there are healthy and unhealthy ways to manage tough emotions like anger. It's not healthy or fair to allow your frustration to ruin everyone else's experience too. The "Managing Big Emotions" chapter (page 67) will help you work through uncomfortable emotions in a healthy way. When can you practice having a positive attitude?

Super-Duper Important:

It takes a strong person to recognize their own weaknesses. Remember, nobody's perfect. We all have strengths and weaknesses. And clearly one of your strengths is your commitment to being the best person you can be!

Friendship Truth #2: Everyone develops friendship skills at a different pace.

The next chapter, "The Friendship Pyramid," describes the different levels of friendship and the skills that lead to healthy friendships. The pyramid also reveals some of the mysteries of friendship, like why some friendships feel different than others and how friendships change over time.

Chapter 3

The Friendship Pyramid: From BFF to NRF (Not Really Friends)

Have you ever noticed that it's easy to be yourself with a certain friend and share your feelings and thoughts? And with another friend you may feel nervous and more careful about what you say and do?

That's because all friendships are different. The Friendship Pyramid illustrates the different phases of friendship and the qualities of each.

FRIENDSHIP PYRAMID

FRIENDSHIPS HAVE DIFFERENT PHASES AND CHANGE OVER TIME.

ALL WE CAN REALLY CONTROL IS OURSELVES. BE THE TYPE OF FRIENDS YOU WANT TO HAVE!

CHANGE

MISUNDERSTANDINGS

CLOSE FRIENDS
Harder to find

- Try to find fair solutions
- Are accepting
- Are fun to be with
- Are trustworthy—share thoughts, emotions, and secrets not shared with friends you don't know or trust as well
- Make you feel comfortable and safe

FRIENDS
(classmates, team members, neighbors)

- Try to find fair solutions
- Are accepting
- Are fun to be with
- Don't share as many secrets as close friends
- Might not know you as well as your close friends so you may not feel as comfortable

AQUAINTANCES
and possible new friends

Undiscovered friendships are always out there! Stay open to meeting new friends

NOT REALLY FRIENDS (NRF)

 Be cautious and kind

- Are nice to you some days, mean other days
- Are untrustworthy—gossip and spread rumors
- Are unaccepting—leave you feeling uncomfortable being yourself
- Are unsafe— ask you to do things you feel uncomfortable with

IMPORTANT: Everyone changes!
Over time, NRF's can learn friendship skills.

Sometimes, a secret needs to be shared with a trusted adult if it's about an unhealthy or dangerous situation. If a secret is about anyone's safety, including yours, it's time to talk to an adult.

Close Friends

The top of the Friendship Pyramid, *Close Friends*, is small and may only include one or two friends. That's because close friends are harder to find, and these friendships usual-ly take longer to develop. Don't worry if you haven't found any close friends yet; many kids may not have any until middle school or even later.

Some friendships may grow into close friends as kids develop stronger friendship skills. And many friendships may never grow into close friends—and that's okay too.

My close friend(s) or people who have qualities I like and may pursue as possible close friends are: _____

_____

_____

_____

_____

_____

Friends

The *Friends* level of the Friendship Pyramid is wider than the tip and includes a variety of friends, like classmates, team members, and neighbors. These friendships are accepting and fun, but they may not feel as comfortable as close friendships. So you might not share secrets or some thoughts and feelings until more trust is developed. Some of these friendships may grow into close friends over time.

My friends or people who have qualities I like and may pursue as possible friends are: ___

_____

_____

_____

Acquaintances & Possible New Friends

The base of the pyramid is wide and filled with possible new friends. Acquaintances are people you don't know very well, but you see them around town or school. For example, an acquaintance could be a girl you've never been in class with, so you don't know much about her. Stay open to meeting new friends. You never know, that girl may grow into a friend someday!

My possible new friends are: _____

_____

_____

Not Really Friends (NRFs)

Friendship skills take practice and a certain level of maturity. NRFs haven't developed some of these skills yet.

This doesn't mean NRFs are bad people or that they can't change. We all learn friendship skills at our own pace. Sometimes, kids with NRF behaviors are struggling with things in their lives, such as self-esteem or family issues. Over time, most NRFs learn how to be good friends. In the meantime, be kind and cautious.

Super Duper Important:

Sometimes, when a girl behaves like an NRF, girls band together and turn against her. This ends up multiplying mean behavior. Yuck! If you decide to move out of an NRF relationship, be sure not to bring others into the situation. It's possible to move away from difficult relationships respectfully by not spreading gossip or turning others against her.

Friendship Truth #3:
Friendships have different phases and change over time.

Friendship Truth #4:
Close friendships can be hard to find and may not happen until middle school or later.

Super-Duper Important:

Friendship is a choice. If you have an un-healthy friendship, you may choose to work with that friend to improve your friendship or take a break from that friendship. A friendship may not be right for you now, but it may be right for you again in the future with time and maturity. Stay open.

Friendships change over time and move up and down the Friendship Pyramid. Maybe your friend moves away. Or you meet a new friend that grows into a close friend. Or you and your friend grow apart for a while. At some time or another, everyone goes through these changes. The "Making New Friends" and "Taking Care of Myself" chapters (see pages 109 and 115) can help when friendship changes are hard.

Chapter 4

What Qualities Do I Like in Friends?

Everyone's drawn to different qualities in friends. One girl may look for a friend who thinks just like she does, while another girl may prefer someone who thinks very differently. One girl may want an energetic friend, while someone else may prefer a calm friend.

It all comes down to personal preference. We're drawn to certain qualities more than others, and that's okay. What's important is that we treat everyone with kindness and as we would like to be treated.

The Magic Friend Machine

Imagine you found a magic machine that could create a brand-new friend. You simply tell the machine what qualities you would like in a friend and . . . *POOF*, your new friend appears. (Qualities are descriptive traits, like kind, honest, adventurous, etc.)

Think about the qualities you'd program into the machine for your ideal friend. Make sure these qualities describe the friend's personality or behaviors that are important to you, not her appearance.

Instructions: Circle the friendship qualities that are important to you from the list below. Feel free to add other qualities to the list.

Friendship Qualities

(Circle the Qualities Important to You)

Accepting	Caring
Active	Cheerful
Adventurous	Compassionate
Brave	Confident
Careful	Cooperative
Calm	Creative

Encouraging   Motivated

Energetic   Neat

Fair   Optimistic

Friendly   Patient

Fun   Peaceful

Funny   Positive Attitude

Generous   Respectful

Genuine   Trustworthy

Good Listener   Unique

Hard Working   Other:_____

Healthy   Other:_____

Helpful

Honest

Independent

Joyful

Kind

Leader

On the lines below, write the three friend qualities MOST important to you:

What Type of Friend Am I?

Have you ever wondered what your friends like most about you? If you had to guess what qualities your friends like about you, what would they be? On the lines below, write three qualities that your friends like about you.

Qualities my friends like MOST about me:__

Friendship Truth #5:
Some girls with strong
friendship qualities may
not have the "most"
friends. Sometimes girls
with the "most" friends
do not make the "best"
friends.

Everyone has certain qualities that they are
drawn to in friends. Keep an eye out for friends
that have the qualities you find important in
friendship. And, of course, being a good friend
is the best way to attract and keep friends too.

Chapter 5

"Oops, I Wish I Hadn't Said That"—Managing Big Emotions in Healthy Ways

One way to attract and keep friends Is to be a good friend. But we all goof up! Sometimes we say or do things in our friend-ships that we regret. This often happens because we experience a big emotion and react without thinking.

Ashley and Natalie's Story:

Ashley and Natalie have been best friends since third grade. They always sit together at lunch and hang out after school. In fifth grade, Monique started hanging out with them too. Ashley really likes Monique, but Natalie's not so sure about a new friend joining their twosome.

One day, Natalie was feeling left out. She pulled Ashley aside and told her she wouldn't be her friend anymore if she stayed friends with Monique. Then she stormed off. Ashley was confused and hurt. Natalie felt horrible too. After school, Natalie talked to her mom about what happened. Talking about her feelings helped her figure out what to do.

Here's what Natalie said to Ashley the next day:

"Ashley, I shouldn't have said I wouldn't be your friend anymore if you're friends with Monique. I'm really sorry. Sometimes I feel left out, but I'll try to find a better way to talk about it next time."

Because Natalie took responsibility for her words and sincerely apologized and Ashley accepted the apology, the friendship was repaired. The incident even helped the girls better understand each other and share their feelings in the future.

Big emotions—like anger, fear, and sadness—can be really uncomfortable. But even uncomfortable feelings are okay. In fact, all emotions are okay. It just takes practice to manage uncomfortable emotions so you can respond in a healthy way.

Steps to Manage Uncomfortable Emotions in a Healthy Way:

1. **Pause:** When you feel an uncomfortable emotion, pause and notice the feeling in your body (racing heart, face feels hot, bellyache, etc.). This sounds easy, but it can be really hard to notice big emotions the moment you are having them.

2. **Breathe:** Take some deep breaths. This'll help you calm down.

3. **Work Through The Emotion:** Instead of avoiding big emotions or letting them get out of control, work through them. Some healthy ways to work through uncomfortable emotions include:

- **Take a break and relax in a calming place**

- Go for a walk or exercise

- Talk to an adult or friend about your feelings

- Write about your feelings in a journal

4. **Respond:** Once your head is clear and you're feeling calm, you can figure out how you'd like to respond.

Unhealthy Ways to Manage Uncomfortable Emotions:

- Say or do something mean to get back at the person who hurt or angered you

- Storm off or throw a fit

- Completely avoid the emotion and pretend you're not having it

How Do I Manage Uncomfortable Emotions?

What emotions feel uncomfortable to you? __

List some ways that might help you work through uncomfortable emotions when they arise. ----------------------------------

----

Friendship Truth #6:
Everyone makes mistakes.

With practice, we get better at managing uncomfortable emotions and choosing a healthy
response. When we mess up in our friendships,
it's important to recognize our mistake, sincerely apologize, and try not to make that
mistake again.

Super-Duper
Important:

Have you ever heard an apology that
seemed insincere? A sincere apology heals,

while an insincere apology can make matters worse. To make sure your apology is sincere, take responsibility for your actions. Let your friend know what you wish you'd done instead and how you'll do things differently next time. Your friend may or may not be able to accept your apology right away. Give her time to process her big feelings too.

Natalie's apology: "Ashley, I shouldn't have said I wouldn't be your friend anymore if you're friends with Monique (taking responsibility). I'm really sorry (sincere apology). Sometimes I feel left out, but I'll try to find a better way to talk about it next time" (what she'll do differently next time).

Chapter 6

Speaking Up with "I Power" When Your Friend Isn't Treating You the Way You Want to Be Treated

Olivia and Grace's Story: Unbalanced Friendship

Olivia and Grace are BFFs. Most of the time they get along pretty well, but the past few months, Olivia has been feeling frustrated. When the girls are deciding what to do, Olivia feels like Grace doesn't listen to her. To keep the peace, Olivia goes along with what-ever Grace wants. As her feelings of anger and sadness grow, Olivia begins to wonder if Grace is really a friend at all. Olivia's mom suggests that she write down her options on how to handle the situation. Here's her list:

- Option 1: Do nothing . . . maybe the problem will go away.

- Option 2: Explode the next time it happens . . . yell or cry, whatever works best.

- Option 3: Stop hanging out with Grace and find a new friend.

- Option 4: Speak up and work to solve the issue with Grace.

All friendships, even close ones, hit bumps in the road. So what did Olivia do?

Olivia decided to try option 4, speak up and work to solve the issue with Grace. Olivia realized that maybe Grace didn't know how much this was frustrating her. Even though speaking up felt scary, Olivia thought it was her best option to improve the situation.

Speaking Up in Friendships with "I Power"

Speaking up in friendships means sharing your feelings and needs with your friend to help resolve problems. By addressing issues (instead of avoiding them), we make things better.

Some girls have no trouble speaking up, but for many, speaking up is really scary. What if your friend doesn't listen? Or she gets mad at you? Or even worse, what if your friend decides not to be your friend anymore?

Yes, speaking up can feel scary, but it's important, and here's why:

We teach others how we want to be treated.

If Olivia never tells Grace how she's feeling, the situation will not change. Olivia will continue to feel unheard and frustrated. And the friends may grow apart. The good news is there's a way to speak up that works best in friendships. We like to call it "I Power" because it involves speaking up for yourself instead of blaming and criticizing others.

How to Speak Up to Connect (Instead of Divide)

Words matter . . . a lot! The words you choose can make matters a lot better or a lot worse. Saying the right words takes practice, but once you learn, it's a tool that will improve friendships your whole life!

Here's how it works:

"I Power"–What to Say	Important Notes
"I feel _____(feeling) when you _____ (behavior)"	Start by sharing your feelings using "I," because when you start with "you" (like, "you hurt my feelings"), your friend may get defensive and stop listening.
because _____ (why)."	Stick to the specific behavior that happened or keeps happening. When you pull in a lot of other stuff, it might get too overwhelming to solve all at once.
"I would like you to _____(request)."	Use a calm, confident tone of voice. Your tone and body language are as important as your words.

So here's what Olivia said to Grace during a calm, private moment:

"Grace, can we talk about something? I feel frustrated when you don't listen to my ideas because I have good ideas too, and it doesn't feel fair. I would like us to take turns when we choose what to do."

Notice that Olivia started with the word "I" instead of "you." This is "I Power," and it increases the chances she'll be heard.

When we start tough conversations with "you," like *you always choose,* it makes the other person feel like they are being attacked and need to defend themselves. And when they're defending themselves saying, *"that's not true,"* they're no longer listening to you.

Imagine if Olivia had said this to Grace instead:

"Grace, we need to talk. You always choose what we do! If you don't stop, I'm going to stop hanging out with you."

How do you think Grace would have responded? If Olivia starts with "you" instead of "I" and doesn't share her feelings, the entire tone of the conversation changes.

"You" Words that Divide	"I Power" Words that Connect
THREATS: "If you _____, I won't _____!" (be your friend anymore, like you, invite you) ACCUSATIONS or BLAME: "You *always*_____!" (get to choose, go first, etc.) "You *never* _____!" (text me, listen, etc.)	SHARING FEELINGS & REQUESTS: "I feel _____ (feeling) when you_____ (behavior) because _____ (why). I would like you to _____" (request)

Yes, even with "I Power," speaking up can feel scary. But remember, we teach others how we want to be treated. Addressing issues that are hurting the relationship is an important part of keeping friendships healthy.

Practicing "I Power"

Describe a situation when a friend repeatedly treated you in a way that you do not like to be treated: _____

_____

_____

Fill in the blanks with how you might have responded with "I Power:"

I feel _____ (feeling)

when you _____(behavior)

because _____ (why).

I would like you to _____ (request).

How do you think your friend would have responded if you said that during a calm, private moment? _____

The next time a friend isn't treating you the way you want to be treated, consider using your "I Power." Before you speak to your friend, practice what you plan to say with a trusted adult or facing a mirror. Be sure to use a calm tone of voice.

When you feel ready, find a time that gives you and your friend privacy and a quiet moment. Be sure to talk face-to-face and not via email, DM, or text. Texts and DM's are easily misunderstood.

When to Use "I Power": Use "I Power" with friends to address behaviors that are hurting the friendship, especially behaviors that happen over and over (such as not listening, not telling the truth, or not treating you respectfully).

When NOT to Use "I Power": If you think your friend will make fun of you or make you feel bad for sharing your feelings, you may choose not to. In relationships that feel unsafe, instead say something like, "I want you to stop gossiping about me" or "I don't like it when you make fun of me. It's time to stop."

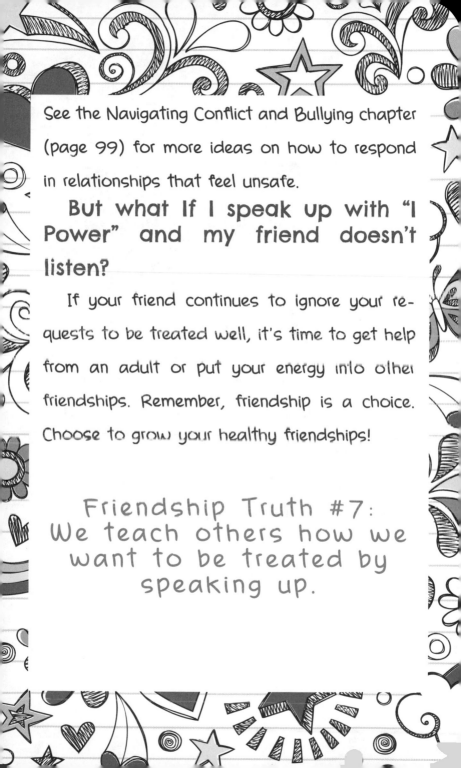

See the Navigating Conflict and Bullying chapter (page 99) for more ideas on how to respond in relationships that feel unsafe.

But what If I speak up with "I Power" and my friend doesn't listen?

If your friend continues to ignore your requests to be treated well, it's time to get help from an adult or put your energy into other friendships. Remember, friendship is a choice. Choose to grow your healthy friendships!

Friendship Truth #7:
We teach others how we want to be treated by speaking up.

Super-Duper
Important:

Learning to stick-up for ourselves in
relationships is one of life's important
lessons. Friends are not mind readers.
If we ignore the behaviors that really
bother or hurt us, nothing will change.

Chapter 7

Tricky Friendship Scenarios: What Would I Do?

Have you ever had a tricky friendship problem that left you unsure of what to do? The stories below were shared by girls who felt the same way. We gathered ideas from other girls about how they'd deal with each situation. As you'll see, there's no right answer. When things get tough in friendship, it's most important to respond in a way that feels right to you.

How would you respond in each of these tricky friendship scenarios?

Marissa's Story: Stuck in the Middle

Marissa has two good friends that don't get along. The three girls hang out at school, but it often ends with the two friends fighting and Marissa feeling frustrated and stuck in the middle. She likes both of these friends and has no idea how to make the situation better.

Luckily, there are several ways to solve any problem. Marissa's task is to think about her options, then find a solution that feels right for her.

Here's how some other girls would tackle this tricky situation:

- I'd try to stay out of the fight and go hang out with other friends until they solve their problem. (Luciana)

- I'd try to come up with a solution, like maybe flipping a coin. (Macy)

- First, I'd figure out if I'm part of the problem. If not, I'd let them figure it out and not get involved. (Lexi)

- I'd talk to an adult to help me figure out what to do. (Shandra)

So what did Marissa do?

Marissa invited some other girls to hang out with her and her two friends. Interestingly, the two girls got along a little better in the larger group. But when they did fight, Marissa gave them space to solve their problem while she and the other girls did something else.

What would you do if you were feeling stuck in the middle like Marissa?_____

_____

_____

Lexi's Story: Haunted by Gossip

Lexi's good friend likes to gossip, but gossiping makes Lexi feel bad. Lexi also wonders what her friend says about her when she's not around. Because her conversations with this friend don't feel safe, Lexi's nervous to speak up and ask her friend to stop gossiping. She's not sure what to do.

Here's how some other girls would tackle this tricky situation:

- If my gossipy friend was really nice, I might still hang out with her, but I'd find other friends too. And I'd try to remember that it doesn't matter what people think of me. It only matters what I think about myself. Maybe she's more of a "friend" than a "close friend." (Violet)

- I'd find a new friend and not hang out with my friend that gossips. I'd try to forget that she might be talking about me too. (Olivia)

- I'd ask her to stop talking behind people's backs. If that didn't work, I'd find other friends to hang out with. (Kendis)

- I'd tell her how I feel and if she didn't listen, I'd find another friend I trust. (Payton)

- When she gossips, I'd just ignore it and change the subject to something else. (Madison)

So what did Lexi do?

The next time her friend started to gossip, Lexi calmly let her know that she feels bad when she talks about people when they're not there. She then changed the subject to something fun. Lexi realized she might need to do this many times before her friend stopped gossiping, so she's going to give it some time to see if it solves the problem.

What would you do if your good friend liked to gossip? _____

_____

_____

Ella's Story: Cheater, Cheater Pumpkin Eater

Ella's friend sits next to her in class and copies her work. If Ella covers her work, her friend makes her feel bad for not sharing her answers. Ella likes this friend but feels that copying is wrong. She's not sure what to do.

Here's how some other girls would tackle this tricky situation:

- I'd ask my teacher to move my desk to a different spot. (Charlotte)

- I'd tell her that she should do her own work because my answers might not be right, and she might know the right answer. (Freya)

- I'd say, "I know you're really smart and you can do this work yourself." (Lexi)

- I'd use my "I Power" and say, "I feel nervous when you copy my work because it's against school rules and it's not helping you learn. I want you to stop." (Izzy)

So what did Ella do?

Ella realized that this friend was not treating her the way she wanted to be treated. She practiced her "I Power" at home, so the next time her friend tried to copy her, she was ready to respond. Later that week, Ella said, "I feel nervous when you copy my work because it feels wrong. I want you to stop." She was surprised at how calm and confident she sounded speaking up. Her friend was surprised too and has not copied her work since.

What would you do if your friend copied your schoolwork? _____

_____

_____

_____

Payton's Story: Inflexible Friend

Payton's friend hardly ever listens to her ideas. Hanging out with this friend leaves her feeling frustrated and ignored. She's tried asking her to include her ideas several times, but it hasn't helped. She's not sure what to try next.

Here's how some other girls would tackle this tricky situation:

- I'd say, "Since we've been doing your ideas for a while, can we try my ideas now?" (Madison)

- I'd say, "Hey, can we try my idea today?" If she says no, I'd remind her that we've been doing mostly her ideas lately. If that doesn't work, I'd find another friend to hang out with that day. (Jala)

- A couple of years ago, I had this friend that always wanted things her way. So I told her to stop, and she did. (Zoey)

So what did Payton do?

Payton realized that when she spoke to her friend about this problem, she didn't use her "I Power." She usually said something like, "You always choose! It's not fair." This made her friend get defensive and respond with, "I do not!"

So Payton practiced her "I Power." The next time her friend was ignoring her ideas, Payton said, "I feel frustrated when we hang out because you don't listen to my ideas. I'd like us to take turns." Her friend listened for a while, but then started ignoring her ideas again. Payton decided to take a break when this happened.

What would you do if your friend didn't listen to your ideas? _____

_____

Macy's Story: Copycat Friend

Macy's best friend likes to dress like Macy, draw what Macy draws, and do whatever Macy wants to do. This has started to bother Macy. She wishes her friend would be herself and express her own ideas. Macy's afraid to hurt her friend's feelings and isn't sure what to do.

Here's how some other girls would tackle this tricky situation:

· I'd remind myself that she copies me because I have good ideas. (Payton)

· I'd tell her that I'm a unique person and she is too and that being the same doesn't show our uniqueness. (Marissa)

· I'd try to have her share her ideas first. Then I'd share different ideas so both of our unique ideas come out. (Lakin)

· This happens with my brother a lot. I let him decide first so he doesn't always copy me. (Maria)

So what did Macy do?

Macy realized that her friend might copy her because she might not have a lot of self-confidence. When Macy was little, she was the same way. So Macy started to encourage her friend and tell her that she liked hearing her ideas. Since Macy's friend didn't think she was a good artist, she continued to copy Macy's drawings. But, her friend did start to develop her own fashion style, thanks to Macy's encouragement.

What would you do if your friend always wanted to be the same as you?

Friendship Truth #8: When things get tough in friendship, it's important to respond in a way that feels right to you.

Remember, there are many ways to solve sticky friendship situations. To find a solution that feels right to you, make a list of your options.

Once you've listed all of your options, decide which one feels best. Then give it a try. If it doesn't work, try another option. Friendship is a journey with challenges along the way. Facing challenges, instead of avoiding them, helps to improve your friendships!

Chapter 8

Navigating Conflict and Bullying

Conflict is unavoidable, especially in the pre-teen and teen years. Maybe your friend shared your secret, and now gossip is spreading about you. Or you were not invited to a friend's party. Or, something you said was misunderstood and caused drama.

As we learned from the Friendship Pyramid, misunderstandings and change are part of friendship. We all make mistakes and say or

do things we wish we hadn't. And sometimes,
kids are mean on purpose. All of this adds up
to painful situations that are hard to navigate!

So, what do you do?

To start, it helps to get a clear understanding of the problem. Conflict is often confused
with bullying, but there is a difference.

Conflict Versus Bullying

Conflict: A struggle or clash between people.

Conflict is common. Most of the stories in this book fall into this catego-
ry. A rude comment, feeling excluded, hurting someone's feelings, posting
an unflattering photo without consent, and disagreements are just a few
scenarios that create conflict.

Bullying : When a person or group repeatedly harasses or harms someone unlikely to defend themselves. The person bullying tends to have more social or physical power
than the person being bullied.

With the growth of technology, bullying has expanded online. Cyberbullying
uses technology—such as social media, text messages, email, or websites—
to humiliate, threaten, or degrade another person.

Whether it's conflict or bullying, ALL of these
situations are difficult!

When it comes to conflict, there is no "right" response. After you think about your options, respond in a way that feels right to you. Here are some ways to navigate conflict.

Ways to Respond to Conflict

- Take care of yourself and your emotions so you can think more clearly. (see Chapters 5 and 10)

- Think about both sides of the conflict to understand your role. Situations are often more complicated than they appear.

- Apologize for your actions as needed.

- Stand up for yourself while being respectful of others.

- Respond with "I Power." (see Chapter 6)

- Choose a response that doesn't add more meanness to the situation.

- Choose not to get involved. Some issues you may decide to drop because they are less important to you. Or you may want to see how things unfold and decide later.

- Talk with a trusted adult to figure out what to do.

Navigating conflict is not easy. If you decide to speak with the person you are in conflict with, practice what you plan to say so you are calm and confident.

Then, find a private time and place to talk. Be sure not to involve others in the conflict. Your goal is to speak your truth, take responsibility for your part, and treat others with dignity. This is no easy task, but an important skill to practice over time.

Ways to Respond to Bullying

Bullying behavior needs to be stopped, and adult assistance may be necessary. If you experience or witness bullying, here are some ways to respond:

- Get help from a trusted adult (school counselor, teacher, parent). Report the issue confidentially if you fear a backlash.

- Stand up tall and give a neutral response so you don't add more meanness to the situation.

- Stay calm and walk away to a crowded place or help the target leave the situation.

- Remind yourself (or the target) that you don't deserve this, and it's not okay!

Neutral responses: (Use a calm, confident voice so you don't give the person bullying your power.)
"I want you to stop."
"I don't need to listen to this."
"Wow, that's really unkind."
"Sorry you're having a bad day."
"I'm just going to ignore that comment."
"Boy, that's some negative energy."

Super-Duper Important:

Be sure to get help from a trusted adult if bullying behavior continues. Remember, nobody deserves to be treated this way. Adults can help remove information that has been shared online and make changes to help you and others feel safe.

Jenna's Story: Dumped by Her Friends

Jenna and her friends have been pals for years. But in sixth grade, things changed. Jenna noticed that her friends would roll their eyes and snicker when she sat down with them. They didn't seem to want her around anymore and even avoided her sometimes.

Jenna was confused and hurt. She had no idea what she had done or what she should do. She kept hoping things would get better, but they didn't. They got worse. Her friends started sharing secret jokes that Jenna knew were about her. And they started to leave mean notes about her around school.

Jenna told her mom about her friends' behaviors a few times, but her mom didn't take it seriously. She thought Jenna was exaggerating. But when Jenna stopped wanting to go to school, her mom finally listened.

She made an appointment for Jenna to talk to the school counselor. With the help of the counselor, Jenna explored her options and decided to stand up for herself. The next time they laughed at one of their "secret Jenna jokes," Jenna stood tall and in a calm voice said, "Wow, that's really unkind." Then she walked away.

Starting over with friends was hard, but Jenna realized that she deserved to be treated with dignity. It took some time, but she did find a new friend. And this friendship felt real because it was filled with kindness and acceptance.

What Would You Do?

Read the following scenarios and write a response that would work best for you in that situation. Feel free to use any of the responses shared in this chapter or make up your own. You may notice that reading them makes you feel uncomfortable. By doing this exercise, you'll be better prepared if any of these situations ever happen.

WHAT WOULD YOU DO?

Scenario 1: A former friend is spreading rumors about you. Now some kids won't even speak to you. _____
_____
_____
_____

Scenario 2: There's a kid in your class that's picked on a lot. Lately a few kids in your class have been making fun of him and calling him names. They start up again when the teacher leaves the room. _____
_____
_____
_____

Scenario 3: A friend had a party and didn't invite you. It seems like almost everyone else in your friend group was invited.
_____
_____
_____

Scenario 4: Describe a conflict you have experienced or witnessed and how you would respond if it happened again. _____
_____
_____
_____

Chapter 9

Making New Friends

Sophie's Story: Always the New Kid

"My mom has a job that makes our family move almost every year. I've been to four schools already. Just when I get used to a new town, new school, and new friends, I have to start over.

I get really worried each time I start a new school. I wonder how hard it'll be to meet new friends. I wonder if the kids at my new school will like me. But even though my stomach's all tied in knots, I try to smile and be friendly. I figure nobody wants to be friends with a grump. The first few days are kind of lonely and awkward, but then it gets better and I meet some new friends."

Making New Friends

At some time or another, everyone needs to make new friends. Possibly your best friend moves away, or you realize a close friendship is unhealthy. Starting over and finding new friends can feel scary, so here are some tips to help:

- Know what kind of friend you want to have and be that kind of friend
- Be friendly: Smile, say hello and ask questions to get to know kids.
- Do things you enjoy to meet people: Take a class, join a team, etc.

What to Say When You Meet Someone New

Say you join a team and don't know anyone, or you're at a party and only know the host—how do you start a conversation with someone you don't know?

- Say "hello" and smile.
- Ask some questions. *(How long have you been playing soccer? How do you know the birthday girl?)*
- Listen.
- Share about you.

Making New Friends: What Would You Do?

Read each scenario below and write what you'd do in that situation to meet someone new. Remember, people are drawn to positive, friendly people, so smile and say hi! And most kids love to share about themselves, so asking questions is a great way to start a conversation.

New Kid on the Team: You start a new sport and don't know anyone on the team. All the other kids seem to know each other really well. _____

_____

_____

_____

Time for a New Friend: You realize that your best friendship is unhealthy and you need to take a break for a while. It's time to make a new friend. _____

_____

_____

_____

Birthday Party Awkward Moment: Your mom drops you off at a birthday party and the only person you know is the birthday girl, but she's really busy. _____

_____

_____

_____

No Friends in Class: It's the first day of school and you end up in a class with a bunch of kids you don't know. ____

_____

_____

_____

Super-Duper Important:

Everyone has to start over and make new friends at times. Use this time to think about what qualities you like in friends and what qualities friends like in you. Explore your interests, join a team, or take a class to meet new friends too.

Chapter 10

Taking Care of Myself During Rough Patches

Friendships are wonderful, but they can also be hard. Even the best friendships have rough patches. How do you take care of yourself when you're feeling blue?

Daphne's Story: Hidden Feelings

"My family's really cheerful, which is mostly awesome. But when I was feeling sad or frustrated, like when school's really hard, I didn't know what to do. I thought bad feelings were bad and that I shouldn't be having them. So I hid my feelings from my family and pretended everything was okay. But eventually the feelings would burst out and surprise everyone."

Taking care of your emotional health

When we're hurt or sick, we know to apply a band-aid, visit a doctor, or rest. But when we feel big emotions like sadness, anger, or loneliness we forget to take care of ourselves. Taking care of our emotional health is just as important as taking care of our physical health.

Here are some ways girls take care of themselves when they're feeling low:

- I talk to my aunt. She's really good at listening and making me feel better. (Miranda)

- I write in my journal. When I write my feelings down, it helps me to sort them out. (Kali)

- I take my dog for a walk and get some exercise. (Nahla)

- I relax in my room and put on my favorite songs. (Claire)

- I draw or do an art project. Being creative makes me feel calm and gives me time to think. (Chloe)

Daphne's Story: Hidden Feelings, Continued . . .

"Last year, a lady visited my class and talked about emotions. She talked about all types of feelings and explained that every emotion is okay, even the tough ones. She helped us think of ways to manage tough emotions in healthy ways. So now, when I notice I'm bottling up my feelings, I write in my journal instead. This helps me get the feelings out and start to feel better."

Create Your Own "Taking Care of Me" Ritual

What makes you feel better when you're feeling down? Creating a ritual to take care of your emotional health helps in tough times. A ritual is a set of activities done in a certain way. Possibly talking with a trusted adult and then taking a bubble bath will help you begin to feel better? Or maybe going for a jog and then writing in your journal?

What ritual would help you take care of yourself when you're feeling low? _____

_____

_____

_____

Celebrate You

It's helpful to remember your many special qualities when you're feeling low. Copy the following page, decorate it, fill in the blanks, and hang it in your room.

UNIQUELY ME!

One positive quality I have is: _____

Something I do well is: _____

Something I feel good about is: _____

_____

Something special about me is: _____

_____

Three things I'm grateful for are: _____

_____

A person who always makes me feel better about

myself is : _____

Super-Duper Important:

All emotions, even the uncomfortable ones, are okay. Emotions make us human after all. Create a ritual that helps you feel better when you're blue. Taking care of your emotional health is an important part of staying healthy!

FRIENDSHIP TRUTH #9: YOU CHOOSE WHICH OF YOUR FRIENDSHIPS TO GROW. GROW THE HEALTHY ONES!

Chapter 11
Putting It All Together

Making and keeping friends takes effort, but it's worth it. Friends add fun and laughter to life. And friends support and accept us, just as we are.

We covered a lot in this book and explored many hidden truths of friendship. Hopefully these truths will help guide your friendships now and in the future. Here's a quick review:

Nine Friendship Truths

- Friendship Truth #1: Healthy friendships feel safe and accepting.

- Friendship Truth #2: Everyone develops friendship skills at a different pace.

- Friendship Truth #3: Friendships have different phases and change over time.

- Friendship Truth #4: Close friendships can be hard to find and may not happen until middle school or later.

- Friendship Truth #5: Some girls with strong friendship qualities may not have the "most" friends. Sometimes girls with the "most" friends do not make the "best" friends.

- Friendship Truth #6: Everyone makes mistakes.

- Friendship Truth #7: We teach others how we want to be treated by speaking up.

- Friendship Truth #8: When things get tough in friendship, it's important to respond in a way that feels right to you.

- Friendship Truth #9: You choose which of your friendships to grow. Grow the healthy ones!

Remember, all friendships have ups and downs and change over time. All you can really control is yourself by being the type of friend you want to have. Keep this book handy as it will help to navigate bumps in the road.

Friends are like stars, you don't always see them, but you know that they're out there. When you practice healthy friendship skills, you're sharing your best self with others. This helps you feel good about yourself and helps others shine too. You've got this. Shine on!

Bonus Friendship Ideas

School Back-up Plan: If you find yourself alone at lunch or recess what can you do? Keep a bag in your backpack with a book, journal, colored pencils, and a few small games. If you don't find a friend to hang out with, just pull something fun out of your bag.

Game Idea Cards: If you and your friends waste a lot of time deciding what to do, make some game idea cards. Write the names of your favorite games on some cards. Be sure to add in some new ideas too. The next time the group has trouble deciding what to play, just pick a card.

Decide How to Decide: It's helpful for groups of kids to agree on a fair way to decide what to do when there are many ideas. Here are some fair ways to decide:

- Majority Rules—Vote and the idea with the most votes wins.

- Alternate Who Decides—For smaller groups, a different person can decide each day (for example, Jodi decides on Monday, Shay decides on Tuesday, etc.).

- Play Each Game for a Short Time—Equally split time playing each game (for example, Tag for ten minutes then Four Square for ten minutes).

Bookclub Discussion Questions:

1. (Chapter 2) Friendship skills take practice. Which friend-ship skills are easy for you? Which skills are harder for you to do?

2. (Chapter 3) The Friendship Pyramid illustrates that friend-ships change, people change, and misunderstandings are common. Think of one of your friendships that moved up or down the pyramid. Was this change easy or hard for you? Explain.

3. (Chapter 5) All emotions are okay, even the uncomfort-able ones. Do you do anything to take care of yourself when you are experiencing an uncomfortable emotion?

4. (Chapter 6) Do you find it easy or difficult to speak up when a friend isn't treating you well? If difficult, what keeps you from speaking up? If speaking up is easy for you, what have you learned along the way?

5. (Chapter 8) Sometimes people confuse conflict with bul-lying. How common is conflict at your school? How common is bullying?

6. (Chapter 8) Do kids know how to respond when they see or experience bullying at your school or online? What would help?

7. (Chapter 9) Making new friends can be tricky. Share a time that you made a new friend. Where and how did you meet?

8. (Chapter 11) The book explores nine friendship truths, which are summarized in the last chapter. What friendship truth is especially helpful to you and why?

9. (Chapter 11) Take a look at the list of friendship truths. Would you add any truths to the list? What would you add?

10. (Chapter 11) What friendship truth do you wish you had learned earlier? Why?

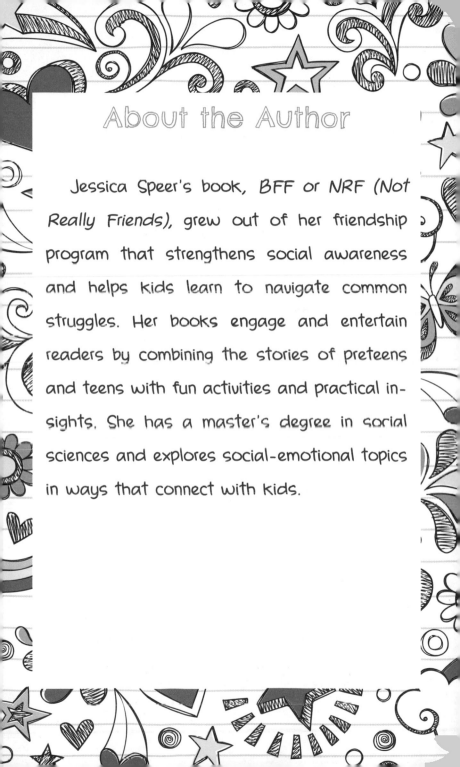

About the Author

Jessica Speer's book, *BFF or NRF (Not Really Friends)*, grew out of her friendship program that strengthens social awareness and helps kids learn to navigate common struggles. Her books engage and entertain readers by combining the stories of preteens and teens with fun activities and practical insights. She has a master's degree in social sciences and explores social-emotional topics in ways that connect with kids.

About Familius

Visit Our Website: www.familius.com

Familius is a global-trade publishing company that publishes books and other content to help families be happy. We believe that the family is the fundamental unit of society and that happy families are the foundation of a happy life. We recognize that every family looks different, and we passionately believe in helping all families find greater joy. To that end, we publish books for children and adults that invite families to live the Familius Ten Habits of Happy Family Life: *love together, play together, learn together, work together, talk together, heal together, read together, eat together, give together* and *laugh together*. Founded in 2012, Familius was located in Sanger, California.

Connect

Facebook: www.facebook.com/familiustalk

Twitter: @familiustalk, @paterfamilius1

Pinterest: www.pinterest.com/familius

Instagram: @familiustalk

FAMILIUS

The most important work you ever do will be within the walls of your own home.